I0105747

COMPLETE
LESSON PLAN
OUTLINES

Alfred J. Liotta, Ed.D., M.S.W.

Former Principal
Bronx, New York
Stamford, Connecticut

Senior Lecturer
Mercy University
New York

Second Edition

Copyright 1986
All Rights Reserved

Alfred John Liotta
Printed in U.S.A

Copyright © 2025 by Alfred J. Liotta, Ed.D., M.S.W.

All rights reserved. No part of this publication may be reproduced, distributed, or transmitted in any form or by any means, including photocopying, recording, or other electronic or mechanical methods, without the prior written permission of the copyright owner and the publisher, except in the case of brief quotations embodied in critical reviews and certain other noncommercial uses permitted by copyright law. For permission requests, write to the publisher, "Attention: Permissions Coordinator," to the address below.

Studio of Books LLC

5900 Balcones Drive Suite 100

Austin, Texas 78731

www.studioofbooks.org

Hotline: (254) 800-1183

Ordering Information:

Special discounts are available on quantity purchases by corporations, associations, and others. For details, contact the publisher at the address above.

Printed in the United States of America.

ISBN-13: Softcover   978-1-964928-73-9
          Hardback   978-1-964928-74-6
          eBook   978-1-964928-75-3

Library of Congress Control Number: 2025911792

This Second Edition Of

COMPLETE LESSON PLAN OUTLINES

Is Dedicated To

Lorraine V. Aponte

Laura G. Neff

And to the legions of dedicated
teachers who have devoted their
lives to preparing our youth to be
productive members of society.

Table of Contents

ABOUT THE AUTHOR

Alfred J. Liotta, Ed.D., M.S.W., the author of When Students Grieve: A Guide to Bereavement in the Schools, 1st and 2nd editions, served in public education in New York City for 32 years, and has written numerous manuals, curricula, and published articles. He is a Certified Pastoral Bereavement Counselor, and he is a parish and program facilitator in the Archdiocese of New York. He is also certified as a grief counselor and *Fellow in Thanatology* by the international Association of Death Education and Counseling.

Dr. Liotta completed his Doctorate in Education and M.S.W. degrees at Fordham University, and he began to unite his educational carcer experience and counseling skills as a clinical thanatologist and family counselor. He is a New York State *Licensed Mental Health Counselor* and a New York State *Licensed Master Social Worker*. He also holds a certificate in *Teen Counseling - "Passages Program."*

Formerly a practicing school administrator, he continues as a compassionate grief counselor and is the coordinator of various bereavement activities. He is also the Pastoral Bereavement Counselor at various churches in the New York area.

Dr. Liotta writes and lectures frequently Among his more notable events, he was as a guest lecturer at Trinity College in Dublin, Ireland, as well as at the nationally known Bellevue Hospital in New York City.

In June 2013, Dr. Liotta was "invited home" to the State University of New York at Oneonta, his initial Alma Mater, as part of the Distinguished Alumni Lecture Series, to deliver a presentation on his book and has newly developed course on bereavement counseling. Dr. Liotta maintains a bereavement counseling practice in White Plains, New York, and he is listed in "Who's Who in the East" and "Who's Who in Education."

On December 6, 2019, Dr. Liotta was inducted into New York's **Westchester County Senior Hall of Fame** for his record of lifetime community service to others.

A native of Brooklyn, New York, Dr. Liotta is a seasoned educator, counselor, and writer.

Preface:

COMPLETE LESSON PLAN OUTLINES

The key to a productive classroom experience is, of course, a carefully and skillfully prepare lesson plan. This is no accident. It takes time and skill to produce a good "road map" to execute a viable lesson.

Over the last fifty years of teaching experience, the author has seen various "models" come and go. Some with awesome and intimidating terminology. Yet, none have had better success than the basic tenets that are outlined in this presentation. Therefore, it must follow that simple, intelligent, and skillful planning is the key to success in the classroom. One might not be dynamic at all times, but one can certainly be well prepared every single time.

Complete Lesson Plan Outlines was designed, and written, with that end in mind. Each lesson provides the necessary elements for one's teaching success.

Enjoy the contents as you ply your craft with confidence and success.

Alfred J. Liotta, Ed.D., M.S.W.

Planning The Lesson

"Complete Lesson Plan Outlines".

TO THE BEGINNING TEACHER   In your preparation as teachers, you have been taught that a properly prepared and executed lesson plan is at the very heart of the learning process. It is the guide or "road map" for instruction

Each lesson plan outline presented in this manual contains the salient elements which comprise a well-balanced and viable lesson. They are highlighted here for your convenience

DO NOW - The Do Now is a brief, clearly presented, student writing activity. It may contain reinforcement material (review) or material designed to lead into the new topic being presented. It is a short activity and should be promptly checked and corrected.

INSTRUCTIONAL OBJECTIVE   - The Instructional Objective, also known as a Pupil Performance Objective, is a carefully worded statement clearly expressing an intended instructional outcome. The Objective is neither a process nor a procedure, but rather an expression of intended results in terms of student performance. It should be clear, precise, and measurable. The applications used in your lesson should be able to determine (measure) to what extent the student has achieved the intended result.

Some sample *Instructional Objectives* are:

Students will correctly use new vocabulary words in complete sentences.

or

Students will be able to add fractions with like denominators.

or

Students will be able to correctly tell time in Spanish.

MOTIVATION
- The motivation is a brief and simple device to challenge the student, arouse interest, and provoke thought. It may be in the form of a question, statement, or anecdote, and must lend itself directly to the topic being presented. It is best to personalize the Motivation and correlate it to the general interests and abilities of the students. By using an apperceptive base, i.e. by using

previously learned material as a springboard for new learning, the Motivation can effectively lead the lesson as it moves through the phases from Development to *Final Summary*. It is truly the "launching pad" of the lesson.

STRATEGIES

- Teacher Procedures/Student Activities - - This phase of the lesson is comprised of the following three components, Development (Presentation), Medial Summary, and Comprehension. The Development provides the logical and sequential movement that carries the lesson from the Objective to the Comprehension. The format must reflect the Instructional Objective and should consist of boardwork, oral work, and reading and writing activities. Audio-visual aids, role playing, pattern drills, and dialogues may also be used. Great care should be taken to correctly pace the timing and tempo of the presentation. An indispensable part of the lesson is a strategically placed *Medial Summary*. Its purpose is to clear up difficulties and solidify the concepts taught. The material learned is made functional.

The final component in the *Development* is the *Comprehension*. The *Comprehension* exercise is a measurement activity. It affords the student the opportunity to actively use what was learned in class. Boardwork is an essential part of this component and may consist of textbook or teacher prepared exercises. Exercises should be promptly corrected with the class and difficulties immediately resolved.

SUMMARY - In actuality, there are two types of summaries contained in a well-planned lesson, the *Medial Summary* (previously mentioned), and the *Final Summary*. The *Final Summary* is of great importance because it clarifies the concepts taught and is an indicator of the extent to which the Instructional Objective was achieved. It is important to note that while summaries have a distinct purpose and place in the format of the lesson, questions should be entertained and welcomed throughout the lesson.

APPLICATION - The Application component of the lesson affords the student the opportunity to utilize the new material that was presented. Its purpose is to provide practice and enables the students to achieve mastery level while applying their newly acquired skills to current and realistic situations. Although the Application may vary with each subject, the function is abundantly clear - practice makes perfect!

HOMEWORK - The *Homework* is an essential part of every lesson. It serves to reinforce the newly presented material. Assignments should be a written activity and should be clearly defined and functional. The assignment may be given at the beginning of the class or may emerge as a natural outgrowth of the lesson, presented at a logical and appropriate time. It should be presented on a level commensurate with the students' abilities and must be checked on a daily basis. Homework should be explained early in the lesson and the teacher should anticipate and eliminate difficulties in order to insure a clear and challenging reinforcement activity. Teachers may wish to personalize the assignment by providing for individual needs and interests. The *Homework* component is one of the most important parts of a well-planned lesson.

Writing The Plan

CLASS	TEACHER	DATE

DO NOW		TEXT	
		PG(S)	EX.
HOMEWORK		TEXT	
		PG(S)	EX.

Classroom Procedures:

Boards: Attendance: Lateness: Windows: Etc.

Explain the *HOMEWORK*: Review *DO NOW* and *HOMEWORK* promptly.

INSTRUCTIONAL OBJECTIVE
MOTIVATION
STRATEGIES — TEACHER PROCEDURES — STUDENT ACTIVITIES:

STRATEGIES

SUMMARY

EXPLANATION OF HOMEWORK

APPLICATION(S)

MISC.

REGISTER —   ATTENDANCE —

CLASS	TEACHER	DATE

DO NOW		TEXT	
		PG(S)	EX.
HOMEWORK		TEXT	
		PG(S)	EX.

Classroom Procedures:

Boards: Attendance: Lateness: Windows: Etc.

Explain the *HOMEWORK*: Review *DO NOW* and *HOMEWORK* promptly.

INSTRUCTIONAL OBJECTIVE
MOTIVATION
STRATEGIES — TEACHER PROCEDURES — STUDENT ACTIVITIES:

STRATEGIES

SUMMARY

EXPLANATION OF HOMEWORK
APPLICATION(S)

MISC.

REGISTER —   ATTENDANCE —

CLASS	TEACHER	DATE

DO NOW		TEXT	
		PG(S)	EX.
HOMEWORK		TEXT	
		PG(S)	EX.

Classroom Procedures:

Boards: Attendance: Lateness: Windows: Etc.

Explain the *HOMEWORK*: Review *DO NOW* and *HOMEWORK* promptly.

INSTRUCTIONAL OBJECTIVE
MOTIVATION
STRATEGIES — TEACHER PROCEDURES — STUDENT ACTIVITIES:

STRATEGIES

SUMMARY

EXPLANATION OF HOMEWORK
APPLICATION(S)

MISC.

REGISTER —   ATTENDANCE —

CLASS	TEACHER	DATE

DO NOW	TEXT	
	PG(S)	EX.
HOMEWORK	TEXT	
	PG(S)	EX.

Classroom Procedures:

Boards: Attendance: Lateness: Windows: Etc.

Explain the *HOMEWORK*: Review *DO NOW* and *HOMEWORK* promptly.

INSTRUCTIONAL OBJECTIVE
MOTIVATION
STRATEGIES — TEACHER PROCEDURES — STUDENT ACTIVITIES:

STRATEGIES

SUMMARY

EXPLANATION OF HOMEWORK
APPLICATION(S)

MISC.

REGISTER —   ATTENDANCE —

CLASS	TEACHER	DATE

DO NOW	TEXT	
	PG(S)	EX.
HOMEWORK	TEXT	
	PG(S)	EX.

Classroom Procedures:

Boards: Attendance: Lateness: Windows: Etc.

Explain the *HOMEWORK*: Review *DO NOW* and *HOMEWORK* promptly.

INSTRUCTIONAL OBJECTIVE
MOTIVATION
STRATEGIES — TEACHER PROCEDURES — STUDENT ACTIVITIES:

STRATEGIES

SUMMARY

EXPLANATION OF HOMEWORK
APPLICATION(S)

MISC.

REGISTER —   ATTENDANCE —

CLASS	TEACHER	DATE

DO NOW		TEXT	
		PG(S)	EX.
HOMEWORK		TEXT	
		PG(S)	EX.

Classroom Procedures:

Boards: Attendance: Lateness: Windows: Etc.

Explain the *HOMEWORK*: Review *DO NOW* and *HOMEWORK* promptly.

INSTRUCTIONAL OBJECTIVE
MOTIVATION
STRATEGIES — TEACHER PROCEDURES — STUDENT ACTIVITIES:

STRATEGIES

SUMMARY

EXPLANATION OF HOMEWORK
APPLICATION(S)

MISC.

REGISTER —   ATTENDANCE —

CLASS	TEACHER	DATE

DO NOW		TEXT	
		PG(S)	EX.
HOMEWORK		TEXT	
		PG(S)	EX.

Classroom Procedures:

Boards: Attendance: Lateness: Windows: Etc.

Explain the *HOMEWORK*: Review *DO NOW* and *HOMEWORK* promptly.

INSTRUCTIONAL OBJECTIVE
MOTIVATION
STRATEGIES — TEACHER PROCEDURES — STUDENT ACTIVITIES:

STRATEGIES

SUMMARY

EXPLANATION OF HOMEWORK
APPLICATION(S)

MISC.

REGISTER —   ATTENDANCE —

CLASS	TEACHER	DATE

DO NOW		TEXT	
		PG(S)	EX.
HOMEWORK		TEXT	
		PG(S)	EX.

Classroom Procedures:

Boards: Attendance: Lateness: Windows: Etc.

Explain the *HOMEWORK*: Review *DO NOW* and *HOMEWORK* promptly.

INSTRUCTIONAL OBJECTIVE
MOTIVATION
STRATEGIES — TEACHER PROCEDURES — STUDENT ACTIVITIES:

STRATEGIES

SUMMARY

EXPLANATION OF HOMEWORK
APPLICATION(S)

MISC.

REGISTER —   ATTENDANCE —

CLASS	TEACHER	DATE

DO NOW		TEXT	
		PG(S)	EX.

HOMEWORK		TEXT	
		PG(S)	EX.

Classroom Procedures:

Boards: Attendance: Lateness: Windows: Etc.

Explain the *HOMEWORK*: Review *DO NOW* and *HOMEWORK* promptly.

INSTRUCTIONAL OBJECTIVE
MOTIVATION
STRATEGIES — TEACHER PROCEDURES — STUDENT ACTIVITIES:

STRATEGIES

SUMMARY

EXPLANATION OF HOMEWORK
APPLICATION(S)

MISC.

REGISTER —   ATTENDANCE —

CLASS	TEACHER	DATE

DO NOW		TEXT	
		PG(S)	EX.
HOMEWORK		TEXT	
		PG(S)	EX.

Classroom Procedures:

Boards: Attendance: Lateness: Windows: Etc.

Explain the *HOMEWORK*: Review *DO NOW* and *HOMEWORK* promptly.

INSTRUCTIONAL OBJECTIVE
MOTIVATION
STRATEGIES — TEACHER PROCEDURES — STUDENT ACTIVITIES:

STRATEGIES

SUMMARY

EXPLANATION OF HOMEWORK
APPLICATION(S)

MISC.

REGISTER —   ATTENDANCE —

CLASS	TEACHER	DATE

DO NOW	TEXT	
	PG(S)	EX.
HOMEWORK	TEXT	
	PG(S)	EX.

Classroom Procedures:

Boards: Attendance: Lateness: Windows: Etc.

Explain the *HOMEWORK*: Review *DO NOW* and *HOMEWORK* promptly.

INSTRUCTIONAL OBJECTIVE
MOTIVATION
STRATEGIES — TEACHER PROCEDURES — STUDENT ACTIVITIES:

STRATEGIES

SUMMARY

EXPLANATION OF HOMEWORK
APPLICATION(S)

MISC.

REGISTER —   ATTENDANCE —

CLASS	TEACHER	DATE

DO NOW	TEXT	
	PG(S)	EX.
HOMEWORK	TEXT	
	PG(S)	EX.

Classroom Procedures:

Boards: Attendance: Lateness: Windows: Etc.

Explain the *HOMEWORK*: Review *DO NOW* and *HOMEWORK* promptly.

INSTRUCTIONAL OBJECTIVE
MOTIVATION
STRATEGIES — TEACHER PROCEDURES — STUDENT ACTIVITIES:

STRATEGIES

SUMMARY

EXPLANATION OF HOMEWORK
APPLICATION(S)

MISC.

REGISTER —   ATTENDANCE —

CLASS	TEACHER	DATE

DO NOW	TEXT	
	PG(S)	EX.
HOMEWORK	TEXT	
	PG(S)	EX.

Classroom Procedures:

Boards: Attendance: Lateness: Windows: Etc.

Explain the *HOMEWORK*: Review *DO NOW* and *HOMEWORK* promptly.

INSTRUCTIONAL OBJECTIVE
MOTIVATION
STRATEGIES — TEACHER PROCEDURES — STUDENT ACTIVITIES:

STRATEGIES

SUMMARY

EXPLANATION OF HOMEWORK
APPLICATION(S)

MISC.

REGISTER —   ATTENDANCE —

CLASS	TEACHER	DATE

DO NOW		TEXT	
		PG(S)	EX.
HOMEWORK		TEXT	
		PG(S)	EX.

Classroom Procedures:

Boards: Attendance: Lateness: Windows: Etc.

Explain the *HOMEWORK*: Review *DO NOW* and *HOMEWORK* promptly.

INSTRUCTIONAL OBJECTIVE
MOTIVATION
STRATEGIES — TEACHER PROCEDURES — STUDENT ACTIVITIES:

STRATEGIES

SUMMARY

EXPLANATION OF HOMEWORK
APPLICATION(S)

MISC.

REGISTER —   ATTENDANCE —

CLASS	TEACHER	DATE

DO NOW		TEXT	
		PG(S)	EX.

HOMEWORK		TEXT	
		PG(S)	EX.

Classroom Procedures:

Boards: Attendance: Lateness: Windows: Etc.

Explain the *HOMEWORK*: Review *DO NOW* and *HOMEWORK* promptly.

INSTRUCTIONAL OBJECTIVE

MOTIVATION

STRATEGIES — TEACHER PROCEDURES — STUDENT ACTIVITIES:

STRATEGIES

SUMMARY

EXPLANATION OF HOMEWORK
APPLICATION(S)

MISC.

REGISTER —   ATTENDANCE —

CLASS	TEACHER	DATE

DO NOW		TEXT	
		PG(S)	EX.
HOMEWORK		TEXT	
		PG(S)	EX.

Classroom Procedures:

Boards: Attendance: Lateness: Windows: Etc.

Explain the *HOMEWORK*: Review *DO NOW* and *HOMEWORK* promptly.

INSTRUCTIONAL OBJECTIVE
MOTIVATION
STRATEGIES — TEACHER PROCEDURES — STUDENT ACTIVITIES:

STRATEGIES

SUMMARY

EXPLANATION OF HOMEWORK
APPLICATION(S)

MISC.

REGISTER —   ATTENDANCE —

CLASS	TEACHER	DATE

DO NOW		TEXT	
		PG(S)	EX.

HOMEWORK		TEXT	
		PG(S)	EX.

Classroom Procedures:

Boards: Attendance: Lateness: Windows: Etc.

Explain the *HOMEWORK*: Review *DO NOW* and *HOMEWORK* promptly.

INSTRUCTIONAL OBJECTIVE
MOTIVATION
STRATEGIES — TEACHER PROCEDURES — STUDENT ACTIVITIES:

STRATEGIES

SUMMARY

EXPLANATION OF HOMEWORK
APPLICATION(S)

MISC.

REGISTER —   ATTENDANCE —

CLASS	TEACHER	DATE

DO NOW		TEXT	
		PG(S)	EX.
HOMEWORK		TEXT	
		PG(S)	EX.

Classroom Procedures:

Boards: Attendance: Lateness: Windows: Etc.

Explain the *HOMEWORK*: Review *DO NOW* and *HOMEWORK* promptly.

INSTRUCTIONAL OBJECTIVE
MOTIVATION
STRATEGIES — TEACHER PROCEDURES — STUDENT ACTIVITIES:

STRATEGIES

SUMMARY

EXPLANATION OF HOMEWORK
APPLICATION(S)

MISC.

REGISTER —   ATTENDANCE —

CLASS	TEACHER	DATE

DO NOW		TEXT	
		PG(S)	EX.
HOMEWORK		TEXT	
		PG(S)	EX.

Classroom Procedures:

Boards: Attendance: Lateness: Windows: Etc.

Explain the *HOMEWORK*: Review *DO NOW* and *HOMEWORK* promptly.

INSTRUCTIONAL OBJECTIVE
MOTIVATION
STRATEGIES — TEACHER PROCEDURES — STUDENT ACTIVITIES:

STRATEGIES

SUMMARY

EXPLANATION OF HOMEWORK
APPLICATION(S)

MISC.

REGISTER —   ATTENDANCE —

CLASS	TEACHER	DATE

DO NOW		TEXT	
		PG(S)	EX.
HOMEWORK		TEXT	
		PG(S)	EX.

Classroom Procedures:

Boards: Attendance: Lateness: Windows: Etc.

Explain the *HOMEWORK*: Review *DO NOW* and *HOMEWORK* promptly.

INSTRUCTIONAL OBJECTIVE
MOTIVATION
STRATEGIES — TEACHER PROCEDURES — STUDENT ACTIVITIES:

STRATEGIES

SUMMARY

EXPLANATION OF HOMEWORK
APPLICATION(S)

MISC.

REGISTER —   ATTENDANCE —

CLASS	TEACHER	DATE

DO NOW		TEXT	
		PG(S)	EX.

HOMEWORK		TEXT	
		PG(S)	EX.

Classroom Procedures:

Boards: Attendance: Lateness: Windows: Etc.

Explain the *HOMEWORK*: Review *DO NOW* and *HOMEWORK* promptly.

INSTRUCTIONAL OBJECTIVE

MOTIVATION

STRATEGIES — TEACHER PROCEDURES — STUDENT ACTIVITIES:

STRATEGIES

SUMMARY

EXPLANATION OF HOMEWORK
APPLICATION(S)

MISC.

REGISTER —   ATTENDANCE —

CLASS	TEACHER	DATE

DO NOW		TEXT	
		PG(S)	EX.
HOMEWORK		TEXT	
		PG(S)	EX.

Classroom Procedures:

Boards: Attendance: Lateness: Windows: Etc.

Explain the *HOMEWORK*: Review *DO NOW* and *HOMEWORK* promptly.

INSTRUCTIONAL OBJECTIVE
MOTIVATION
STRATEGIES — TEACHER PROCEDURES — STUDENT ACTIVITIES:

STRATEGIES

SUMMARY

EXPLANATION OF HOMEWORK
APPLICATION(S)

MISC.

REGISTER —   ATTENDANCE —

CLASS	TEACHER	DATE

DO NOW		TEXT	
		PG(S)	EX.
HOMEWORK		TEXT	
		PG(S)	EX.

Classroom Procedures:

Boards: Attendance: Lateness: Windows: Etc.

Explain the *HOMEWORK*: Review *DO NOW* and *HOMEWORK* promptly.

INSTRUCTIONAL OBJECTIVE
MOTIVATION
STRATEGIES — TEACHER PROCEDURES — STUDENT ACTIVITIES:

STRATEGIES

SUMMARY

EXPLANATION OF HOMEWORK
APPLICATION(S)

MISC.

REGISTER —   ATTENDANCE —

CLASS	TEACHER	DATE

DO NOW	TEXT	
	PG(S)	EX.
HOMEWORK	TEXT	
	PG(S)	EX.

Classroom Procedures:

Boards: Attendance: Lateness: Windows: Etc.

Explain the *HOMEWORK*: Review *DO NOW* and *HOMEWORK* promptly.

INSTRUCTIONAL OBJECTIVE
MOTIVATION
STRATEGIES — TEACHER PROCEDURES — STUDENT ACTIVITIES:

STRATEGIES

SUMMARY

EXPLANATION OF HOMEWORK
APPLICATION(S)

MISC.

REGISTER —   ATTENDANCE —

CLASS	TEACHER	DATE

DO NOW		TEXT	
		PG(S)	EX.
HOMEWORK		TEXT	
		PG(S)	EX.

Classroom Procedures:

Boards: Attendance: Lateness: Windows: Etc.

Explain the *HOMEWORK*: Review *DO NOW* and *HOMEWORK* promptly.

INSTRUCTIONAL OBJECTIVE
MOTIVATION
STRATEGIES — TEACHER PROCEDURES — STUDENT ACTIVITIES:

STRATEGIES

SUMMARY

EXPLANATION OF HOMEWORK
APPLICATION(S)

MISC.

REGISTER —   ATTENDANCE —

CLASS	TEACHER	DATE

DO NOW		TEXT	
		PG(S)	EX.
HOMEWORK		TEXT	
		PG(S)	EX.

Classroom Procedures:

Boards: Attendance: Lateness: Windows: Etc.

Explain the *HOMEWORK*: Review *DO NOW* and *HOMEWORK* promptly.

INSTRUCTIONAL OBJECTIVE
MOTIVATION
STRATEGIES — TEACHER PROCEDURES — STUDENT ACTIVITIES:

STRATEGIES

SUMMARY

EXPLANATION OF HOMEWORK
APPLICATION(S)

MISC.

REGISTER —   ATTENDANCE —

CLASS	TEACHER	DATE

DO NOW	TEXT	
	PG(S)	EX.
HOMEWORK	TEXT	
	PG(S)	EX.

Classroom Procedures:

Boards: Attendance: Lateness: Windows: Etc.

Explain the *HOMEWORK*: Review *DO NOW* and *HOMEWORK* promptly.

INSTRUCTIONAL OBJECTIVE
MOTIVATION
STRATEGIES — TEACHER PROCEDURES — STUDENT ACTIVITIES:

STRATEGIES

SUMMARY

EXPLANATION OF HOMEWORK

APPLICATION(S)

MISC.

REGISTER —   ATTENDANCE —

CLASS	TEACHER	DATE

DO NOW		TEXT	
		PG(S)	EX.
HOMEWORK		TEXT	
		PG(S)	EX.

Classroom Procedures:

Boards: Attendance: Lateness: Windows: Etc.

Explain the *HOMEWORK*: Review *DO NOW* and *HOMEWORK* promptly.

INSTRUCTIONAL OBJECTIVE
MOTIVATION
STRATEGIES — TEACHER PROCEDURES — STUDENT ACTIVITIES:

STRATEGIES

SUMMARY

EXPLANATION OF HOMEWORK
APPLICATION(S)

MISC.

REGISTER —   ATTENDANCE —

CLASS	TEACHER	DATE

DO NOW	TEXT	
	PG(S)	EX.
HOMEWORK	TEXT	
	PG(S)	EX.

Classroom Procedures:

Boards: Attendance: Lateness: Windows: Etc.

Explain the *HOMEWORK*: Review *DO NOW* and *HOMEWORK* promptly.

INSTRUCTIONAL OBJECTIVE
MOTIVATION
STRATEGIES — TEACHER PROCEDURES — STUDENT ACTIVITIES:

STRATEGIES

SUMMARY

EXPLANATION OF HOMEWORK
APPLICATION(S)

MISC.

REGISTER —   ATTENDANCE —

Class Seating Charts

SEATING PLAN

CLASS   PERIOD

CLASS   PERIOD

CLASS   PERIOD

CLASS   PERIOD

SEATING PLAN

CLASS   PERIOD

CLASS   PERIOD

CLASS   PERIOD

CLASS   PERIOD

SEATING PLAN

CLASS   PERIOD

CLASS   PERIOD

CLASS   PERIOD

CLASS   PERIOD

SEATING PLAN

CLASS   PERIOD

CLASS   PERIOD

CLASS   PERIOD

CLASS   PERIOD

Class Record Keeping

FALL SPRING 20			1st Marking Period				2nd Marking Period				3rd Marking Period				Text Avg.	Quiz Avg.	Final Exam	Final Mark
CLASS	Room																	
Period	Register																	
Id No.	Name																	

FALL SPRING 20	1st Marking Period				2nd Marking Period				3rd Marking Period				Text Avg.	Quiz Avg.	Final Exam	Final Mark
CLASS Room																
Period Register																
Id No. Name																

School Directory

Principal: Rm. _____   Phone _____

Asst. Prin. Rm. _____   Phone _____

Dept. Off. Rm. _____   Phone _____

Dean's Off. _____   Phone _____

Library   _____   Phone _____

Cafeteria   _____   Phone _____

Gym   _____   Phone _____

Infirmary   _____   Phone _____

Supply Rm.   _____   Phone _____

Lavatory(s) _____   Phone _____

Security Off. _____   Phone _____

Fire   _____   Phone _____

---------------- _____   Phone _____

---------------- _____   Phone _____

---------------- _____   Phone _____

---------------- _____   Phone _____

www.ingramcontent.com/pod-product-compliance
Lightning Source LLC
Chambersburg PA
CBHW042340030426

42335CB00030B/3412